When I'm Not Myself

Poems In and Out of My Skin

By Kelle Grace Gaddis

ISBN: 978-93-89074-58-1

First Edition: 2019
Rs. 200/-

Cyberwit.net
HIG 45 Kaushambi Kunj, Kalindipuram
Allahabad - 211011 (U.P.) India
http://www.cyberwit.net
Tel: +(91) 9415091004 +(91) (532) 2552257
E-mail: info@cyberwit.net

Printed at Repro India Limited.

"Imagination is the only weapon in the war against reality."

Lewis Carroll, *Alice In Wonderland*

Preface

Some of the poems in *When I'm Not Myself* are true and others are persona poems. I'll let the reader discern what's real or imagined.

Publishing Credits

Knowing What To Keep - Originally published in Interim

Quagmire - Originally published in Interim

Towards Sunset - Originally published in The New Independents

Chasing - Originally published in BlazeVox 15

The Shelves - Originally published in My Myths with Yellow Chair Review

Bones - Originally published in My Myths with Yellow Chair Review

Lost Tribe - Originally published in Clamor

Thinking About How Much They Hate You When They Can't Control You While Shopping At A Discount Store - Originally published by The Dope Fiend Daily

Falling - Originally published in Poetry of Spring's Embrace

Building Happily Ever After - Originally published in Poetry of Spring's Embrace

Contents

Knowing What to Keep

When you went to war,
I wore pearls around my neck.
I counted your years away on it
as if it were a rosary.
We thought war a necessity
for country until your fourth tour,
by then we'd lost our conviction.
The pearls were lost in a move and you,
as if in trade, were brought back to me.
Before you arrived home, the brass
gave me a red, white and blue scarf.
I wore it loosely over my shoulders.
When I ran towards you in the rain
my arms reaching for yours,
it blew off. I let the it lie where it lay,
unwilling to let you go for
a small muddied flag.

Quagmire

In the end I no longer cared about the birds or sky
it was only the density of the Earth pulling me into
itself, the worms, the idea of disappearing entirely,
free from all that once ran through the house, all
that left in misunderstanding, tears, and anger. I am
not home anymore, for I am not me anymore. I am
the last gasp of air from a dream of deep breathing.
One where everything worked out as planned.
You and I were kind and people were friendly,
welcoming, eager to share their love.
In this version, no one broke my heart or your soul
and our spirits never dampened. We were laughter
because laughter is its own music, rising up bright
and lovely, so different than the dead we've become.
We're so different than anything we'd ever hoped
or dreamed. It's like I never knew us at all.
Isn't that a sad song?
I'm sure it is the saddest of songs, playing through
the roots. Funny how the sorrows won't leave me
alone or give us peace, not even here where ashes
mix with rain. All's as stagnant as a quagmire, that
mucky noun to conjure old wars. As I sink into it,
I know the newness knows nothing of our troubles,
I can't blame them for not paying attention.
They're all rushing forward to make what they're
doing feel meaningful, relevant, eternal.

Forgive

Fame, be it fifteen minutes or longer
only makes the ego stronger.
Fashion, whether classical or trendy
hides the body, all image is pretending.
Only love, beauty, and forgiveness are eternal,
If lost in darker souls, it becomes an
untapped internal, They remain black,
bitter, miasmic, and infernal.
All in favor of outrageous displays of rage
will find place in academia or upon political stage.
At home, we navigate more peaceful dealings,
seeing through the eyes of healing. For us,
kisses, flowers, and apologies are true,
we remain open as the sky when blue.
We make peace after battles,
rising higher than those that prattle
about drawing lines they'll never cross,
to me, you would be too great a loss.

Towards Sunset

I am concave today
sunken in the hollow
Missing hangs empty
in the heart space
Hope's light could be lifting,
if it weren't exposing
We were children once
clipped out of ruled paper,
hands gripped tightly,
sisters of a sort
until time, alleged healer,
severed our common
We had laughter in summer,
a wholeness like the sun, it
as a fresh cantaloupe split,
the juicy of the living,
two halves bursting with seeds
We gangly girls dangling
in the Evergreens
Our feet ahead of themselves
running toward sunset,
ever present in our skin, as yet
unable to imagine the end

Chasing

Speaking of rainbows, today's was magnetic. Of course,
absent the rain shouldn't it be called a hallucination? We fell

over ourselves trying to get to the end of it. "The gold!" You
cried, "Is utterly unverifiable," like Don Quixote, except he

chased windmills. I stuttered into numbness wanting to say,
"I'm here!" in spite of the lie in it. Something was not right

about the day, rainbows, or plain-bows, aren't supposed to set
people on edge, yet this one did. At the closest point, you were

red, a deep-hearted, open-veined geyser. I was orange, not a
spray-tan snafu, but naked, moist, like a skinless peach. Oh,

how the others squealed! Their empty hands holding tight to
leprechauns, delirious, drunk on green and blue charging like

donkeys in an indigo dream. Until we fell, spilling our
serpents, crawling after spare change, choked and empty

things, discarded wrappers, broken bottles, evaporated
quixotic arches of ephemeral glee.

There's not enough left in us to say "Goodbye"
So, we lay here in the melting sun,

remembering as if we were together,
having left without saying a word.

The Shelves

Harry refused to listen.
Eventually, he had his ears removed.
He hung shelves where his ears used to be.
His wife wanted to put curious from Hawaii on the shelves,
a hula girl, a ukulele boy.
But, Harry never heard her request.
He placed a salt shaker on one side of his head and
a peppermill on the other.
By nightfall Harry had forgotten the shelves.
At dinner he demanded seasoning for his meat.
His wife pointed to the shelves.
Not understanding her gesture,
he pounded the table with his fists,
until the salt crashed to the floor.
Harry grabbed his wife and shouted,
"Now look what you've done!"

Bones

The moment Zack woke up he knew someone had stolen his bones.
He slid out of bed and hit the floor with a thud.
Bewildered how this could have happened he lay limp on the floor.

He saw dozens of unopened ballots under his bed.
All the votes he never bothered to cast.
Zack knew, no one had stolen his bones.

He'd given them away.
Now he couldn't take a stand
because he had no bones.

Lost Tribe

My crib was a plastic laundry basket.
In it I was swaddled,
tucked into the design of our story.
Mother layered it like sediment, as rich
as the reservation's cliffs I called home.
In time, I'd fall to the stones below.
A kite cut from its tether.
My heritage, drowned in the gene pool.
My memories altered.
My identity, my story,
taken by a sudden light,
a darkroom door opened,
turning partially developed images white

Thinking About How Much They Hate You When They Can't Control You While Shopping At A Discount Store

2019 (consequences be damned) is about standing up for myself
Being honest even if it makes
the control girls eyes bleed
and their intolerance for diverse
opinions trigger the dumping of
word garbage upon my tired

Baskets of questionable eggs,
Totalitarian insanity too heavy
to bare. No, I won't eat their no-
integrity Cheese Wiz and stale

I must be as real as a coffee because
control girls lie like welcome mats
They call their wobbly-cart abuse
green tea and organic fruit

Control freaks hate you when they can't control you
Soft apples with worms gnawing
behind a shiny red or green
I don't eat rot or moldy, none of
their *let us tell you how to be*

Any that cater to the unkind,

diminish themselves. Crate

rats, content beggars starving
at the bitches table, a few blue
bread crumbs, chicken feed
is all they'll ever share –

my God it feels good to give
them the finger. A gesture
as stout as dark lager as joyful
as an exclamation mark at the
end of "Buy one get one free!

Authenticity isn't as risky as cowards say

They long for independence too
even though they'll never be free
range birds. They're the other clucks
all packaged the same, teaming with
toxins on their way to obscurity

I love to scan my own items
In my red laser beeps, I hear
thousands of lost voices each
recognizing worth, shouting,
"No need for a checker here!

Outside I'm hungry but I stop to

buy a raffle ticket for the Arts
I feel optimistic, full of caring

about what's right. And, although

it can’t be proven because the
drawing was weeks away

I believe that’s when I won.

Little Animals

Before nightfall Uncle finds the coins, one for every year since 1800. He held the collection over his head, blocking the light, and told you what happens to thieves.

He blistered your backside with a leather strap until your cracked sobs ceased and you became a young mute swan.

Deprived of shiny things, we play at life. Today we're sister crows plotting, remembering.

Our early wings carry us to the station where we transform again.

Resting cross-legged on the curb, our arms woven through the bars of the wrought-iron fence, invisible as mice to people going places.

The travelers make our stillness ache. At school, I am more eagle than crow, mouse or swan proudly flying above them all.

At Uncle's house, I'm reduced, a frightened fox hiding from the red-coated riders hanging on the walls.

We know that if it weren't the coins, it would've been something else. Our sticky fingers are always trying to find something to hold onto.

I am as guilty as you, having swept tiny boxes of presidents into my pack, coins from the American mint, while you looted a two-century set.

After sundown, we're still scurrying through the streets miles from Uncle's house.

We find colorful stubs of chalk, atop pink, purple, and yellow flowers on the sidewalk, the remnants of other children's happy day.

Close to Uncle's we build ourselves up and strut like cats under the streetlamps casting cones of light, giant golden coins, impossible to carry, in beak or paw.

Outside Uncle's, you find two shiny pennies, a quarter, and a wadded five-dollar bill, fallen money is treasure for little animals like us. As quick as the crack of a whip when you hold the new money high, briefly appearing bigger than Uncle, almost human until the light goes on inside.

Later, we'll line our nest, our den, with cash, deposits in a bank of hope, a light on the altar of happiness below a memory, a family photo, hidden in my suitcase.

You're a baby on mother's lap, and I'm not much more; my hand reaches up to fathers and, although he hasn't grasped it yet when the photo fixes time, I know he takes my hand in his. We look as calm as lion cubs under their care. Someday they'll be back from the hunt, and we'll be well fed.

Our parents were wild beasts to fierce to cage. I hope they'll forgive the barbwire strung around my heart. It's all I have to protect the endangered species I've become. One day, sister and I will become majestic beasts that no one can contain and all the fences raised at Uncle's house will disappear, and we too will run free.

"It would seem that I'm a bad feminist."

~ Margaret Atwood, author of the *Handmaid's Tale*

Walking Past The Single Women With Your Good-looking Man

After you're together a while, after you know he loves you, you
walk past the single women glaring at your good fortune.
You feel them assess your worth to this man that they covet.
It can't be her looks is written on their sad, well-crafted faces.
One whispers, "Nympho" the other "Bjs."
A platitude retort is considered, the one about beauty
being in the eye of the beholder.
I say nothing.
You can't let them know they've cut you with their smoky eyes.
If they knew, they'd take a piece of you.
For all you know, it would be the piece he loves the most.
Instead, you loudly boast, *I can hardly wait until we get home.*
The single women recoil; nasty cats unable to sink their claws.
You glide home, your own tail twitching, your arm locked in his.

Sometimes his love feels too big for your thrice broken heart.
Luckily, every day it overflows the beating chalice, it heals wounds
more seamlessly than Super Glue.
For now, you don't worry about Hula girls or swimsuits.
Your mind will calculate calories and how many pounds-per-week
you can lose tomorrow.

You hope it doesn’t matter.
You pray that your good-looking man is harder to lose than the fat on your inner thighs.
You forgive yourself for your anti-feminist thinking because you love your life, his company, yourself most of the time.
These thoughts are ice cream eaten in secret, slips, honest mistakes; even though you know to get rid of the evidence.
You never hide it all.
Your thoughts join you at the gym, in bed, everywhere.
All because you believe sacrifice is better than being alone.

Falling

In the ivory tower falling is as truth, a misstep
on a broken thought racing quickly
Aristotle insisted heavy things fall faster than
lighter things
No one doubted until Galileo dropped
pebble and stone,
cherry and apple,
side by side,
out a forever leaning
The bigger did not fall harder or faster,
all plummeted in equity

Yet, Aristotle, again, without counting,
declared men have more teeth than women
In spite of his wife's smile, as full as his,
as bountiful as any
Teeth were not counted
A female misfortune, or Aristotle's refusal to
look inside her mouth?
He never did. Instead he made prejudice his
premise. A lack of experimentation or
verification meant nothing to Aristotle,
and everything to Galileo

Today, we remember these men as equals

Hundreds of years later, for equal work,
my paycheck, among men, insists I have
fewer teeth. In spite of my lightness, I fall
faster than they that weigh more. I smile
wide as if numbers could prove my gravity
I bare every tooth as I consider Aristotle's
theories and Galileo's proofs, hoping for a
supernatural surprise, before Earth concludes,
what the envelope hides. My paycheck is
a bad parachute

It, as hollow as Aristotle's philosophical
In his time,
to this day,
I fall
My parachute punctured
A daughter of Galileo
waiting for justice
to function like a gravity,
pulling salaries together,
a force compelling

Building Happily Ever After

Words as anvil, hammer, or nail, strikes
down love, shoddy construction quickly fails.
Gentle speech, forges a golden foundation
Upon it we rise, a two-person nation. No coup
can fell these strong-made walls. We, towers
of laughter, sway but never fall. Save to roll
in humor until tears spill out of joyful eyes,
our happy union is as two pillars of light,
shining brightly, forever growing wise.

Survival of the Fittest

Unravel, run naked into the sea,
a choice to sink or swim, die or be.

Creatures hunger in the deep,
dim sharks, find you tasty meat.

Careful not to lose your feet!
Quick to shore, upon the beach

bait a hook quick waters reach
creeps skulking in the deep.

Catch them, cut them, toss
their bones upon the heap.

Foul bottom fish, quick to blame, eager to
destroy, defame, all above their ugly game.

It's not ours to endure seasickness
Our fortune is survival of the fittest.

Body Shadows

Eyes dry as my last martini
Lips cracked and split
My mouth an empty olive pit
echoes of absinthe and bullshit

My youth's shadow looms confused
an apparition in my glass, infused
Skyy blue the taste of lost dreams

how hollow life can seem. So ugly,
obvious, and strange. My body's
nerves, my mind and brain crave
clarity, a voice beautiful and sane

Ah, there's liquor in my glass,
twirl it, taste it, the cure at last!
Let the specters dance in smoke,
liquids feed my hungry ghost

If I Were ee cummings

When I gets the groove
whisky turns to water
it's an easy trick
drink up my whisky
cause the ice melts quick

When I gets the groove
I talk in tongues
it's an easy trick,
rhythmic around
until I feel sick

When I gets the groove
I'm up all night
?it's an easy trick,
stackin' words like bricks

When I gets the groove
I'm not myself
it's an easy trick
Readin' works 'til
another's tone sticks

If Emily Dickinson Time Travelled To Today And Created A Facebook Profile

This is my post to the world,
    That fails to look on me –
I'm beauty of another time
    As tortured as your sea

These words are quickly gifted
    to hearts I'll never see;
I'll wait behind a white wall
    to see if you like me

If William Blake Were Transported to a Tattoo Parlor in 2020 at The Moment a Mother Catches Her Underage Daughter Getting Rose Sleeves

Ah roses! fixed fast in time,
You've defied the laws of nature:

By drawing inky vines
Where art exists on pale canvas,

her mother now decries,
"Your arms are lost my daughter!"

The girl offers a reply, "Tattoo flowers,
mother, transcend ordinary life.

Morning Joe

Let's talk sugar
sweet and white
into coffee
black as night

Cross my lips
full and red
down my throat
to wake the dead

If you want it
hot and fast,
be sweet to me
or we won't last

CHILL PILLS

short poems by

E. Martin Pedersen

ISBN: 978-93-6354-119-1
Cover Painting on stone by Giselle Treccarichi

First Edition: 2024
Rs. 200/-

Cyberwit.net
HIG 45 Kaushambi Kunj, Kalindipuram
Allahabad - 211011 (U.P.) India
http://www.cyberwit.net
Tel: +(91) 9415091004
E-mail: info@cyberwit.net

Printed at Repro India Limited.

Here I am

alive

HUMAN

BEING

Eccomi

vivo

ESSERE

UMANO

stress stress stress
oh what stress
even the word stress
our lives doomed
by stress, distrcss
dress and undress

stress stress stress
oh che stress
perfino la parola stress
le nostre vite condannate
dallo stress, l'angoscia
il vestirsi e lo svestirsi

head of silver and gold
green trees for hands
sunsets for eyes
he's realized

la testa di argento e oro
alberi verdi come mani
tramonti come occhi
si è realizzato

I'm stripped naked, now what?

mi sono spogliato nudo, e adesso?

if I could fly
land on a cloud
play a little joke on you

se potessi volare
atterrare su una nuvola
ti giocherei uno scherzetto

when freedom is an illusion
then are dreams true
and our daily obligations
a parable of falsity

quando la libertà è un'illusione
allora i sogni sono veri
e i nostri obblighi quotidiani
sono una parabola di falsità

like a new decade
I roll over
and go back to sleep

come un nuovo decennio
mi giro
e torno a dormire

the Cliff House, San Francisco
bought and sold, burnt and rebuilt
tales of deals and trysts
we don't hear over the breaking waves

il Cliff House, San Francisco
comprato e venduto, bruciato e ricostruito
storie di accordi e incontri illeciti
che non sentiamo per le onde che si frantumano

something in that seafood lunch
didn't sit well
barking sea lions in San Francisco Bay

qualcosa in quel pranzo di frutti di mare
mi ha fatto male
leoni marini ruggiscono nella baia di San Francisco

roasted coffee odor
from under the bridge
goodbye hometown

l'odore di caffè torrefatto
da sotto il ponte
addio casa mia

poets staring at the same full moon
all over the world
most of them wordless
most of them not on drugs
go back to their mystery
reading with peppermint tea

poeti che fissano la stessa luna piena
in tutto il mondo
molti di loro senza parole
molti di loro non hanno preso droghe
tornano al loro mistero
da leggere con il tè alla menta

something inside
I can't get out
so I try

c'è qualcosa dentro
che non riesco a fare uscire
perciò ci provo

I changed the last line of my poem
to the present tense
and that makes all the difference

ho cambiato l'ultima frase della mia poesia
al tempo presente
e questo fa tutta la differenza

we sat on the same bench
not speaking
at 2 a.m.

stavamo seduti sulla stessa panchina
senza parlare
alle 2 di notte

every American
boy and girl meet
with a can of beer in their hand

i ragazzi americani e le ragazze
americane si incontrano
con una lattina di birra in mano

I opened the door
you came in without a word
carrying a bag

ho aperto la porta
tu sei entrata senza una parola
portandoti un borsone

I want to hear smell feel your breath
so close I enter your nostrils
I want to live in your lungs
get oxygen to charge me
to roil me with love

voglio sentire odorare toccare il tuo respiro
così vicino che entro nelle tue narici
voglio vivere dentro i tuoi polmoni
prendere ossigeno per caricarmi
per intorpidirmi con l'amore

she on the balcony aching
for love, he tossed her
an apple

lei sul balcone con la voglia
d'amore, lui le tirò
una mela

grandparents after Sunday dinner
the most romantic phrase
"you wash, I'll dry"

i nonni dopo il pranzo domenicale
la frase più romantica
"tu lavi, io asciugo"

I found a gold mask
halfway up the stairs

ho trovato una maschera d'oro
a metà delle scale

stick figures
dancing in circles
around the light bulb

degli omini
ballando in cerchio
attorno alla lampadina

the resistance will burn
without a pressure regulator
to whistle like a tea kettle

la resistenza brucerà
senza un regolatore di pressione
che fischia come un bollitore

he ate too much cauliflower
now he's got brain fever
because her breath smells like
boiled tomatoes
when she groans from deep inside

lui ha mangiato troppo cavolfiore
adesso ha la febbre celebrale
perché l'alito di lei sa di
pomodori bolliti
quando gemiti dal profondo

I cheated on my third wife
with my second wife
which was alright
until she found out —
    which she?
I can't recall

ho tradito la mia terza moglie
con la mia seconda moglie
che andava bene
finché lei non l'ha scoperto
    quale lei?
non ricordo

water carried in my hands
for you to drink now is gone —
divorce

l'acqua che ti ho portato tra le mie mani
per bere adesso non c'è più —
divorzio

www.ingramcontent.com/pod-product-compliance
Ingram Content Group UK Ltd.
Pitfield, Milton Keynes, MK11 3LW, UK
UKHW041317190726
13845UKWH00025B/327

9 789389 074581